GIFTED
&
TALENTED®

*To develop
your child's gifts
and talents*

D1622034

LANGUAGE ARTS

Copyright © 1992 by RGA Publishing Group, Inc., and Susan Amerikaner

All rights reserved. No part of this work may be reproduced or transmitted in any form or by any means, electronic or mechanical, including photocopying and recording, or by any information storage or retrieval system, except as may be expressly permitted by the 1976 Copyright Act or in writing by the publisher.

Manufactured in the United States of America

ISBN 0-929923-85-5

10 9 8

Cover design: Brenda Leach
Cover illustration: Kerry Manwaring

GIFTED
&
TALENTED®

*To develop
your child's gifts
and talents*

LANGUAGE ARTS

A Workbook for Ages 4–6

Written by Susan Amerikaner • Illustrated by Leesa Whitten

Lowell  House
Juvenile
Los Angeles
CONTEMPORARY
BOOKS
Chicago

GIFTED AND TALENTED WORKBOOKS will help develop your child's natural talents and gifts by providing activities to enhance critical and creative thinking skills. These skills of logic and reasoning teach children **how** to think. They are precisely the skills emphasized by teachers of gifted and talented children.

Thinking skills are the skills needed to be able to learn anything at any time. Unlike events, words, and teaching methods, thinking skills never change. If a child has a grasp of how to think, school success and even success in life will become more assured. In addition, the child will become self-confident as he or she approaches new tasks with the ability to think them through and discover solutions.

GIFTED AND TALENTED WORKBOOKS present these skills in a unique way, combining the basic subject areas of reading, language arts, and math with thinking skills. The top of each page is labeled to indicate the specific thinking skill developed. Here are some of the skills you will find:

- Deduction – the ability to reach a logical conclusion by interpreting clues

- Understanding Relationships – the ability to recognize how objects, shapes, and words are similar or dissimilar; to classify and categorize

- Sequencing – the ability to organize events, numbers; to recognize patterns

- Inference – the ability to reach logical conclusions from given or assumed evidence

- Creative Thinking – the ability to generate unique ideas; to compare and contrast the same elements in different situations; to present imaginative solutions to problems

How to Use Gifted & Talented Workbooks

Each book contains activities that challenge children. The activities vary in range from easier to more difficult. You may need to work with your child on many of the pages, especially with the child who is a non-reader. However, even a non-reader can master thinking skills, and the sooner your child learns how to think, the better. Read the directions to your child, and if necessary, explain them. Let your child choose to do the activities that interest him or her. When interest wanes, stop. A page or two at a time may be enough, as the child should have fun while learning.

It is important to remember that these activities are designed to teach your child **how to think,** not how to find the right answer. Teachers of gifted children are never surprised when a child discovers a new "right" answer. For example, a child may be asked to choose the object that doesn't belong in this group: a table, a chair, a book, a desk. The best answer is **book,** since all the others are furniture. But a child could respond that all of them belong because they all could be found in an office. The best way to react to this type of response is to praise the child and gently point out that there is another answer too. While creativity should be encouraged, your child must look for the best and most **suitable** answer.

GIFTED AND TALENTED WORKBOOKS have been written and designed by teachers. Educationally sound and endorsed by leaders in the gifted field, this series will benefit any child who demonstrates curiosity, imagination, a sense of fun and wonder about the world, and a desire to learn. These books will open your child's mind to new experiences and help fulfill his or her true potential.

Draw a line to match each pair of rhyming words to its picture. The first one is done for you.

bug-tug

fat-hat

pup-cup

pet-jet

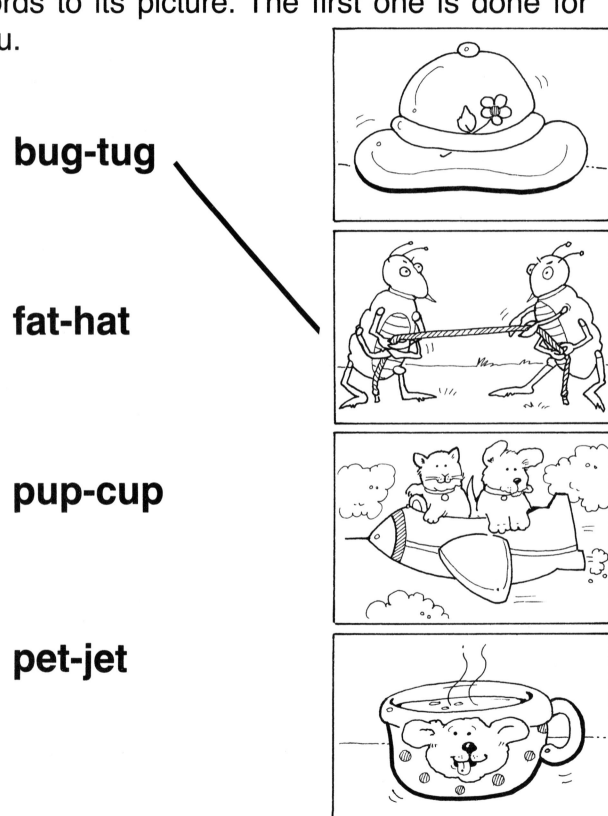

Draw a line to match each pair of rhyming words to its picture.

sea-tea

funny-bunny

snake-cake

sore-door

Think of two words that rhyme and go together to make a silly picture. Write the words and draw the picture.

This is a _____ - _____ .

Here are some words to help you. Try to think of more on your own!

run	top	pop	ball
tall	sun	hug	stop
mop	rock	rug	small
mug	fun	bug	sock

A long time ago people drew pictures to tell stories. Read the story on the rock.

man

river

walk

house

sunny

rain

fish

When pictures are used to stand for words, they are called symbols. Draw your own story with symbols.
(You can use the symbols below and the ones on the page before this one, too.)

bear

hunt

night

grass

hear

run

Make up your own picture symbols. Draw your symbols in the box. Write the words under the symbols. Then draw a story using your symbols.

MY SYMBOLS

Here is my story:

Two words fell into the word machine! They got stuck together and came out as one new word. Look at the new word that came out. Which two words fell in to make this word? Circle the two words.

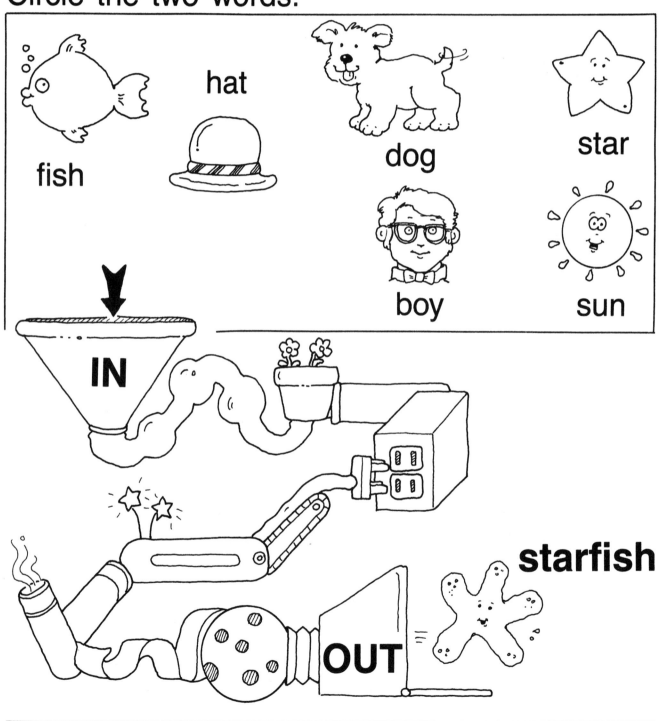

fish

hat

dog

star

boy

sun

IN

OUT

starfish

Circle the two words that fell into the word machine.

house

cat

rain

bird

flower

coat

IN

OUT

raincoat

Four words fell into the word machine. Two new words came out! Circle the four words that fell in.

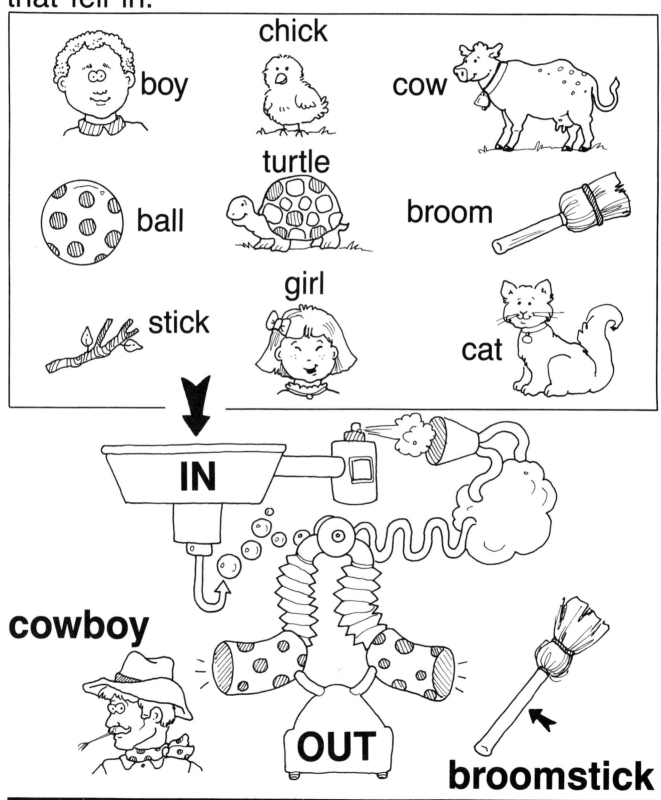

chick

boy

cow

turtle

ball

broom

girl

stick

cat

IN

cowboy

OUT

broomstick

Two words fell into the word machine and came out as one new word. Circle the two words that fell in and draw a picture of the new word they made. Write the word.

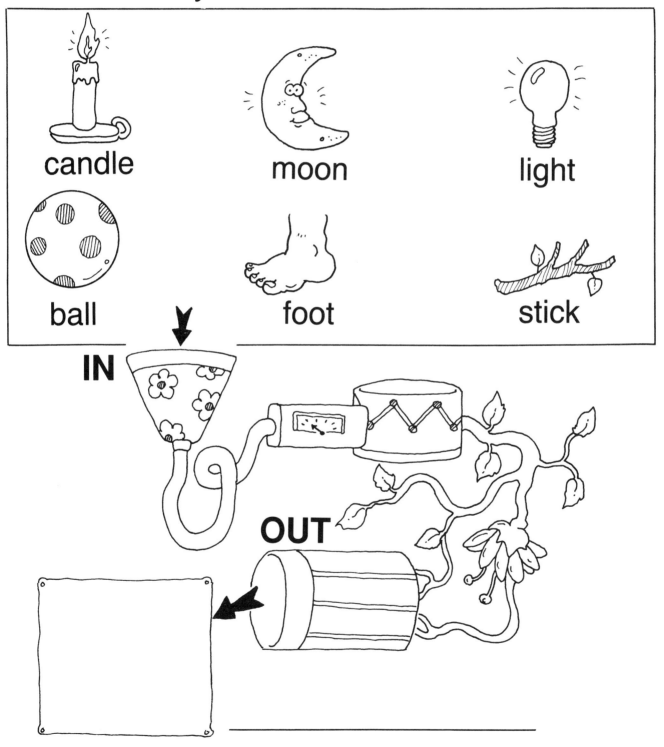

candle

moon

light

ball

foot

stick

IN

OUT

Read the nursery rhyme.

Little Miss Muffet

Sat on a tuffet,

Eating her curds and whey.

Along came a spider,

Who sat down beside her,

And frightened Miss Muffet away!

What do you think Miss Muffet will do <u>after</u> she runs away? Draw a picture of this in the box.

Read the nursery rhyme.

Jack be nimble,
Jack be quick,
Jack jump over
The candlestick.

What do you think Jack will do <u>after</u> he jumps? Draw a picture of this in the box.

Read the nursery rhyme below. Then imagine what Humpty Dumpty was doing <u>before</u> he fell off the wall. Draw a picture of this in the box.

Humpty Dumpty sat on a wall.

Humpty Dumpty had a great fall.

All the King's horses and all the King's men

Couldn't put Humpty Dumpty together again.

Read the nursery rhyme. Then draw pictures to show what Jack and his wife did <u>before</u> and <u>after</u> dinner.

Before:

Jack Sprat could eat no fat,

His wife could eat no lean;

And so between the two of them,

They licked the platter clean.

After:

Find and circle the things you think are wrong in this picture.

Find and circle the things you think are wrong in the shopping mall.

Find the 5 things that rhyme with cat. Circle them.

Read all about Rumpumps.

Rumpumps hate to get out of bed.
They never take a bath.
Rumpumps have a lot of hair.
They are not red or blue.

Draw a picture of a Rumpump.

Read all about Sopnuts.

Sopnuts are good with peanut butter.
They are not round.
Sopnuts are crunchy.
They are bigger than donuts.

Draw a picture of you eating Sopnuts.

Read all about Poozoos.

Poozoos are big.
They are happy.
Poozoos do not like junk food.
They love to play games.

A Poozoo came to visit you. Draw a picture of what happened.

Find the secret word. Read all the clues.
Then write each letter in the correct box.

1. **D** is on top.

2. **G** is under **O**.

Which animal's name did you spell? Color the animal.

Find the secret word. Read all the clues.
Then write each letter in the correct box.

1. **X** is on the bottom.

2. **O** is under **F**.

Which animal's name did you spell? Color the animal.

Find the secret word. Read all the clues. Then write each letter in the correct circle.

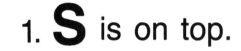

1. **S** is on top.

2. **L** is on the bottom.

3. **E** is on top of **A**.

Which animal's name did you spell? Color the animal.

The turtles have letter names. Read the clues. Then write each letter on the correct turtle.

1. **G** is first.

2. **B** is behind **U**.

Which turtle is last?
What word did they spell?

The hippos have letter names. Read the clues. Then write a letter on each hippo.

1. **T** is **not** wearing a hat.

2. **F** is not next to **T**.

3. Where is Hippo **A**?

What word did the hippos spell? ___ ___ ___

This rainbow is frozen in a block of ice. Draw a picture of what it will look like when it melts.

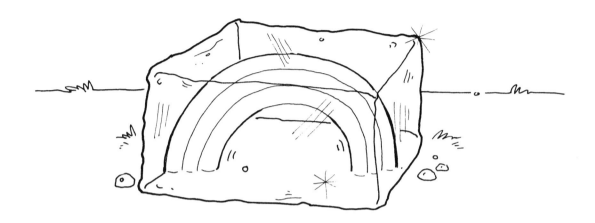

Scientists found this machine on Planet Koop. What do you think it's for? Draw a picture of someone from Koop using this machine.

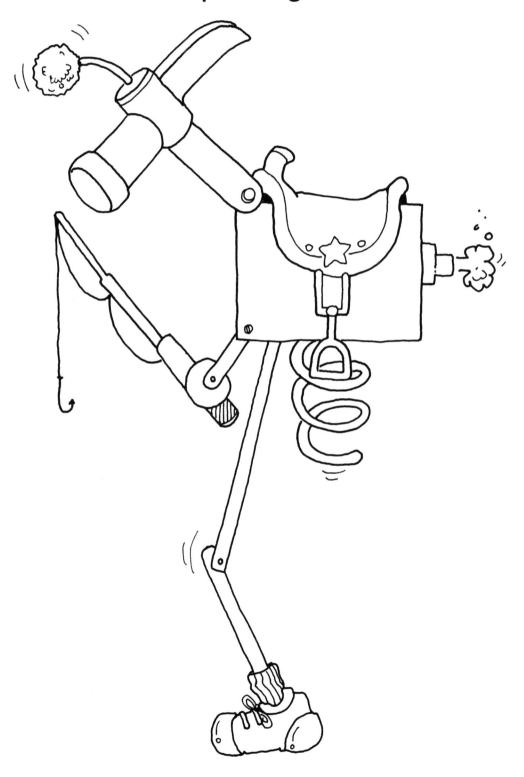

This pot at the end of the rainbow is <u>not</u> filled with gold. It is full of something else. Draw a picture of what you think is in it.

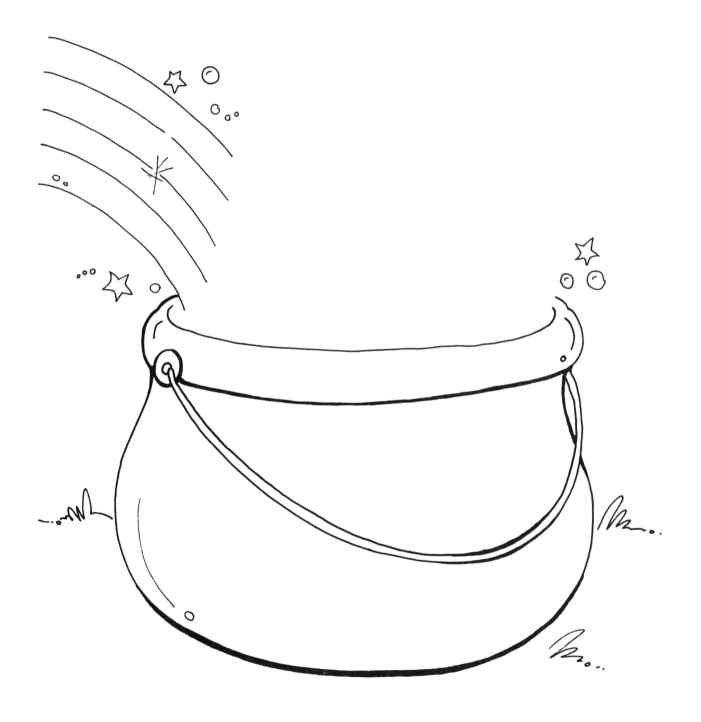

An elephant is in your bathtub! Draw a picture to show how you get it out.

Draw a line from each word to the box that is the same shape as the word. The first one is done for you.

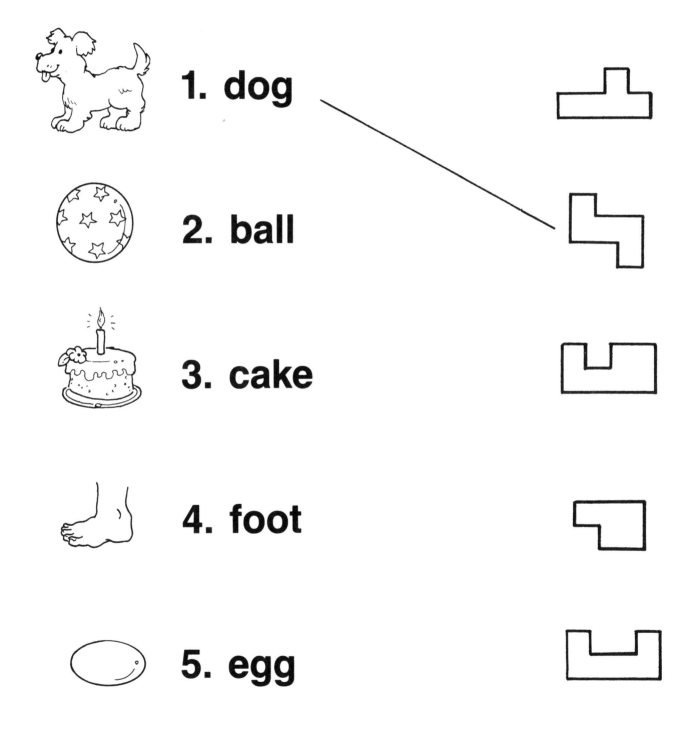

1. dog

2. ball

3. cake

4. foot

5. egg

Draw a line from each word to the box that is the same shape as the word.

1. bug

2. zoo

3. book

4. monkey

5. rabbit

6. puppy

Copy each word into the box that is the same shape as the word. One is done for you.

1. cat

2.

3.

4.

nut   cat   top   doll

Copy each word into the box that is the same shape as the word. Read the message.

bunny the happy is

Draw what each person is thinking.

Draw what each person is thinking.

Use the pictures and words below to fill in this word puzzle.

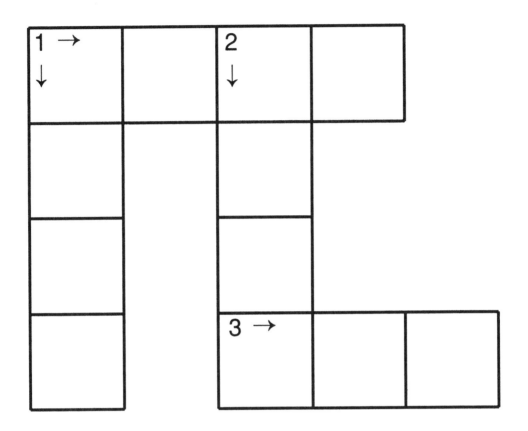

Across →

1. baby

3. top

Down ↓

1. book

2. boat

Use the pictures and words below to fill in the word puzzle.

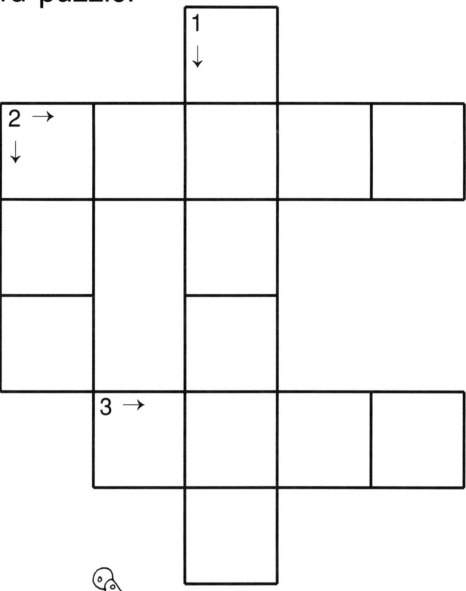

Across →

2. clown

3. neck

Down ↓

1. monkey

2. cup

Use the pictures and words below to fill in the word puzzle.

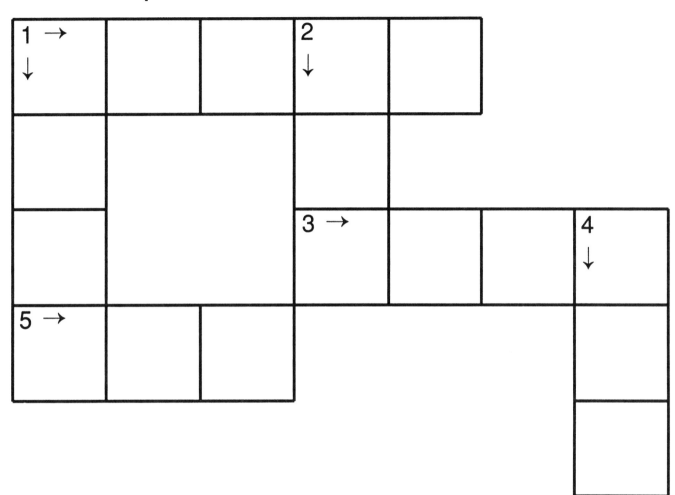

Across →

1. house

3. nose

5. dog

Down ↓

1. hand

2. sun

4. egg

Use the words and pictures below to fill in the word puzzle.

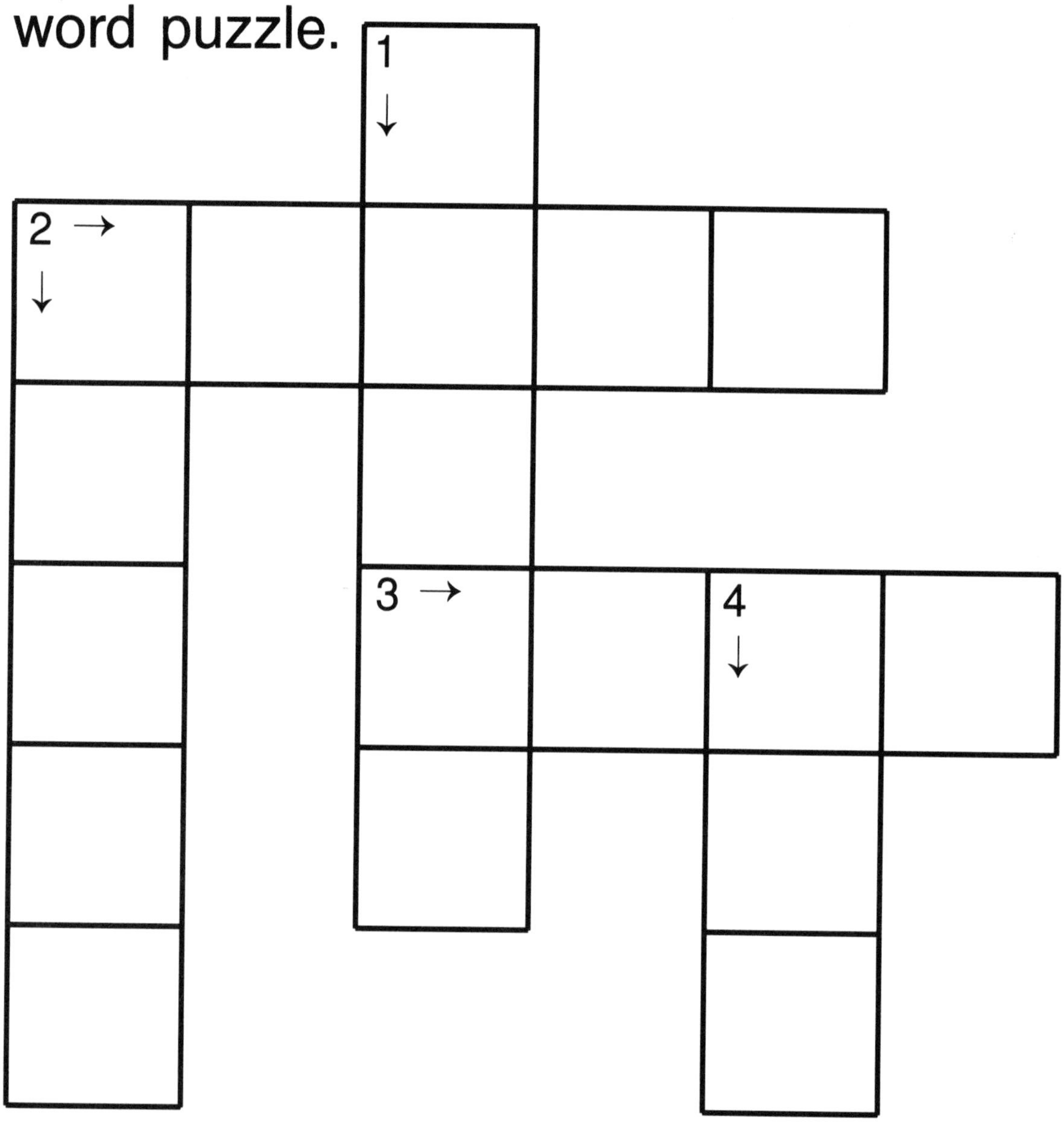

Across →

2. train

3. duck

Down ↓

1. candy

2. tiger

4. cat

Color the M line red.
Color the R line blue.
Color the L line yellow.

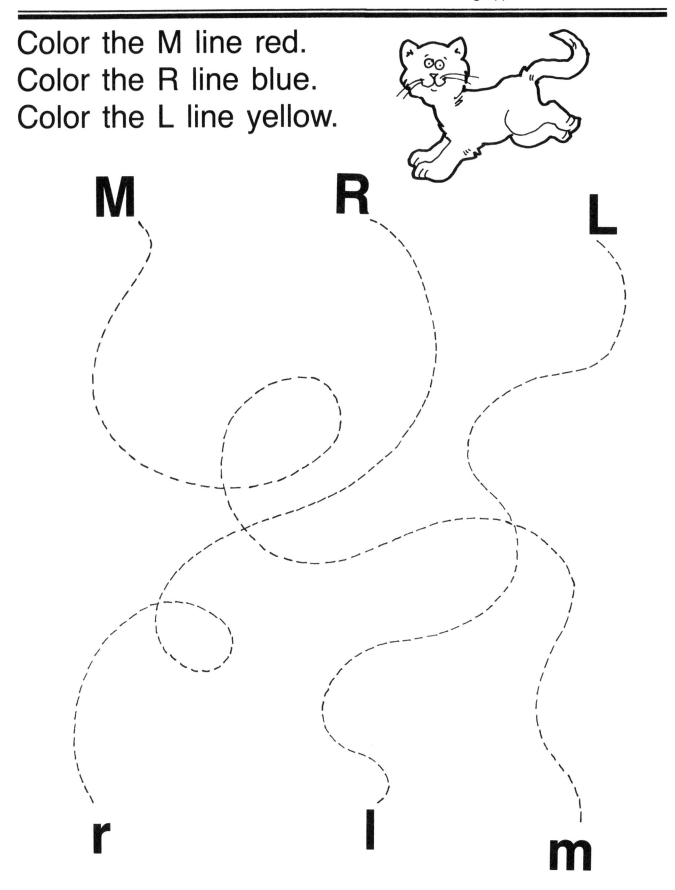

M   R   L

r   l   m

Color the A line blue.
Color the D line green.
Color the B line red.

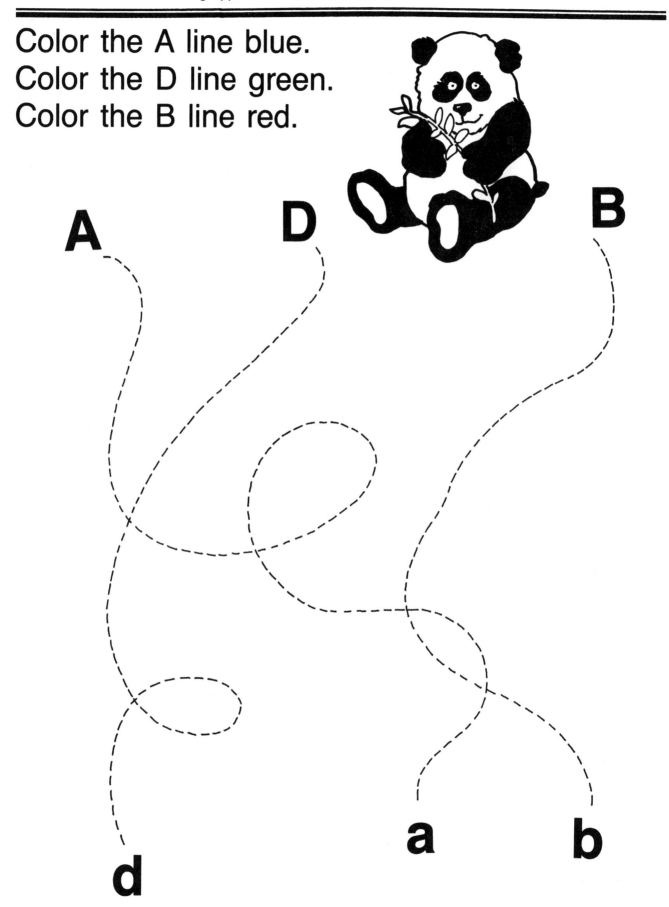

Find out what Henrietta has under her hat.

Cross out all the A-a's.
Cross out all the B-b's.
Cross out all the E-e's.
Cross out all the H-h's.

A f a b A

B e E a H

r b B h A

e o a h g

Which letters are left?
Write them below.

She has a ___ ___ ___ ___ .

What is the parrot saying? Cross out all the letters that come after P in the alphabet.

Q r H R s

T u q e l

R r v w z

I t T x V

R Y o Z

Which letters are left?
Write them in the
spaces above.

Jack planted some more magic beans. But these beans grew down, not up. Draw what Jack found when he followed his new beanstalk.

Draw a line from the whole object to the picture that shows a part of the object. One is done for you.

Draw a line from the part of the object to the whole object.

Find the 4 things that rhyme with **pop**. Circle them.

Use the pictures and the word box to fill in the crossword puzzle.

Across →

2.

3.

Down ↓

1.

2.

Word Box

top	house	hat	bed

53

Use the pictures and the word box to fill in the crossword puzzle.

Across →

1.

3.

Down ↓

1.

2.

Word Box

| boat | hug | bug | baby |

54

Use the pictures and the word box to fill in the crossword puzzle.

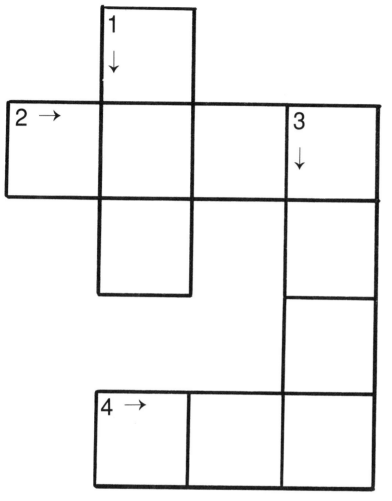

Word Box

ball

car

lion

sun

Across →

2.

4.

Down ↓

1.

3.

Use the pictures and the word box to fill in the crossword puzzle.

Word Box

duck

bird

book

dog

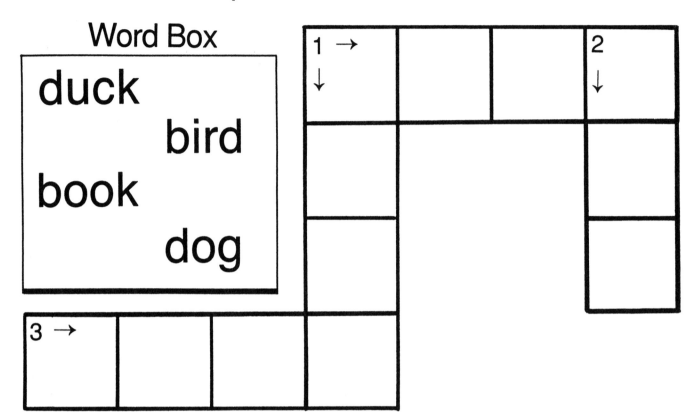

Across →

1.

3.

Down ↓

1.

2.

Look at the pictures. Try to remember how to spell the words. Write them in the puzzle. If you need help, turn back to the word boxes on the pages before this one.

Across →

1.

3.

Down ↓

1.

2.

Look at the pictures. Try to remember how to spell the words. Write them in the puzzle. If you need help, turn back to the word boxes on the pages before this one.

Across →

1.

3.

Down ↓

1.

2.

Find the 5 things that rhyme with **dug**. Circle them.

Here are pictures of people doing things the way they did them a long time ago. Now we have inventions that make it easier to do these things. Draw a line from each box to the invention. One is done for you.

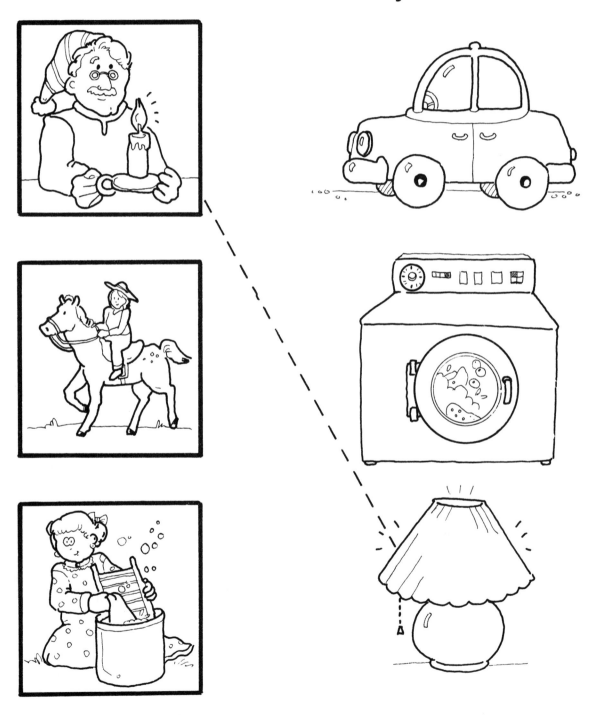

Draw a line from each box to the correct invention.

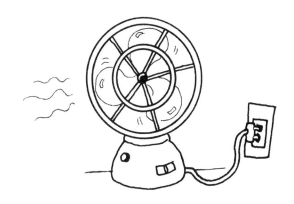

A long time ago cars looked like this:

Now cars look like this:

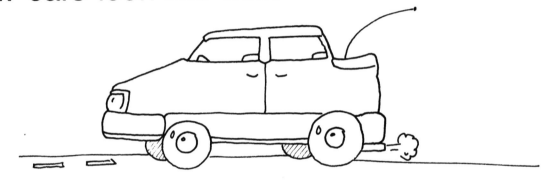

Draw a picture of what you think cars will look like when you're grown up.

A long time ago people dressed like this:

Now people dress like this:

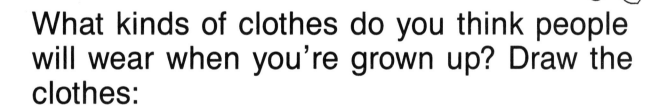

What kinds of clothes do you think people will wear when you're grown up? Draw the clothes:

Draw a line from each object to the picture that shows what is **inside** the object. One is done for you.

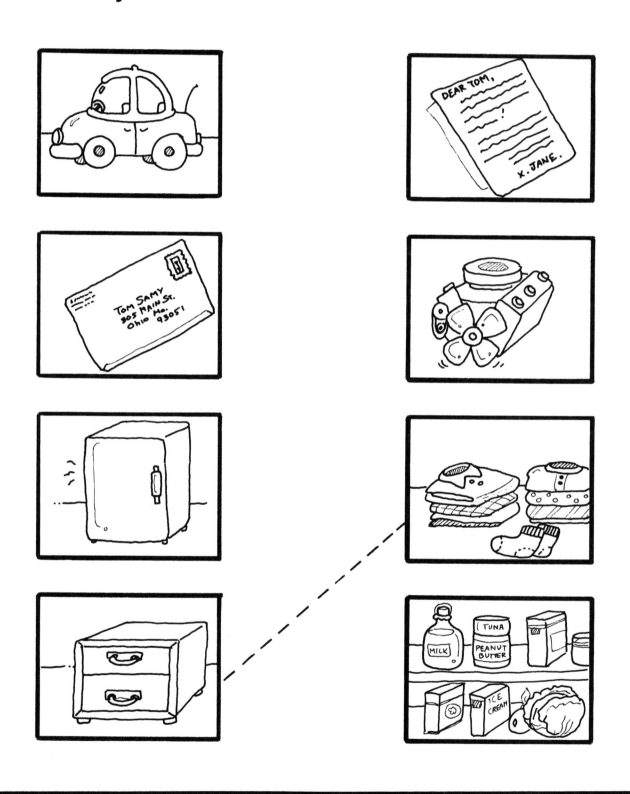

Draw a line from each object to the picture that shows what is **inside** the object.

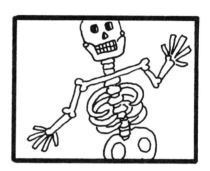

Read this **Good Luck — Bad Luck** story.

1. What good luck! 2. What bad luck!

3. What good luck!

Draw your own **Good Luck — Bad Luck** story.

1. What good luck!   2. What bad luck!

3. What good luck!

Find and circle the things that you think are wrong in this picture.

Look at the words in the box. Find them in the puzzle and circle them. Two are done for you.

UP	CAR	GET
ME	NO	HE

U	P	Q	L	N	G
A	Z	M	X	O	E
M	O	E	S	B	T
H	E	T	C	A	R

Look at the words in the box. Find them in the puzzle and circle them.

BIG   DOG   TO
LOOK   ON   SEE

B	P	R	D	T	T
I	X	U	O	M	O
G	K	P	G	N	Q
L	O	O	K	S	R
S	E	E	V	O	N

Look at the words in the box. Find them in the puzzle and circle them.

FAT	GO	FUN	RUN
DO	TOY	BOX	CAT

C	A	T	R	G	O	T
F	X	X	B	Z	P	O
A	B	P	U	M	D	Y
T	R	U	N	Z	O	X
C	B	T	F	U	N	Q
A	C	O	D	V	R	I
B	R	T	X	M	N	Y

Find and circle the things that you think are wrong in this picture.

Look at all the pictures, one at a time. When you think you can remember them all, turn to the back of this page.

Find the pictures you saw on the page before. Circle **only** those pictures.

Now turn back and check. Did you remember them all?

In this picture there are 6 things that **end** with the letter T. One of these things is circled. Find the other 5 things and circle them.

Imagine using a door 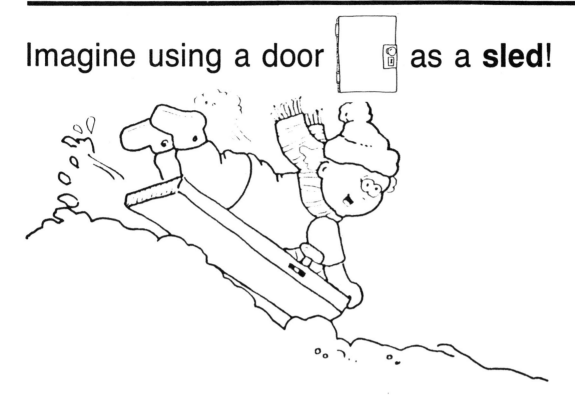 as a **sled**!

It's fun to think of new ways to use things.
Draw a picture of another way to use a door.
You can be silly or serious!

Draw 2 new ways to use a table.

Draw 3 new ways to use a hat.

Suppose a shoe . . . grew? Draw a new way to use this very big shoe.

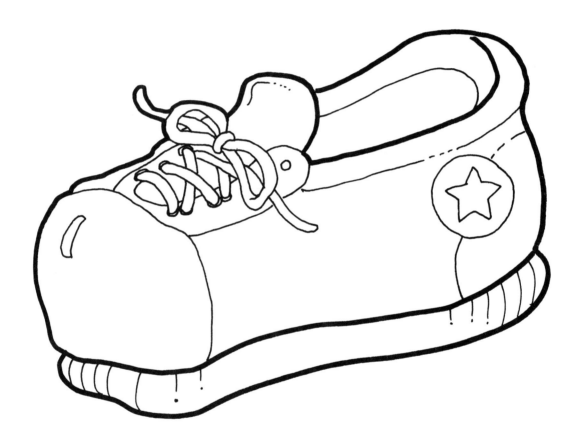

The shoe shrank! Draw 2 new ways to use this tiny shoe.

Find the things that **end** with the letter G. One is done for you. Find 9 more things and circle them.

Draw a line from each letter to the one that will look the same when the missing parts are filled in. Fill in the missing parts. One is done for you.

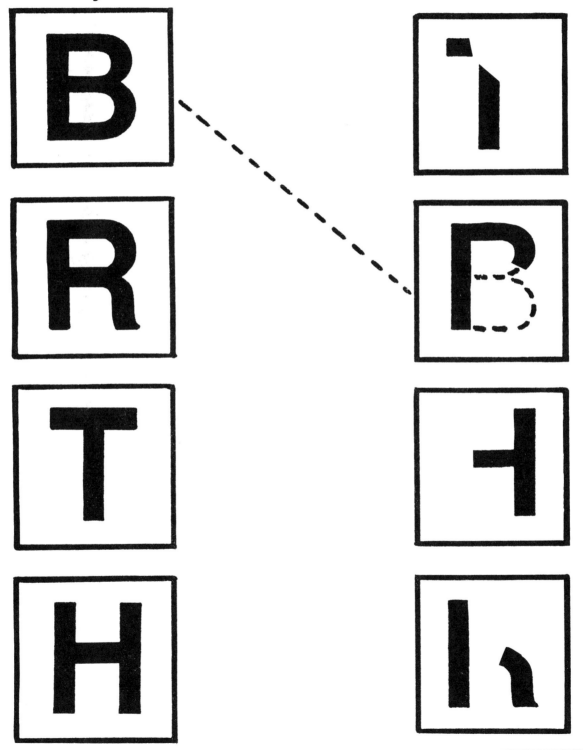

Draw a line from each letter to the one that will look the same when the missing parts are filled in. Fill in the missing parts.

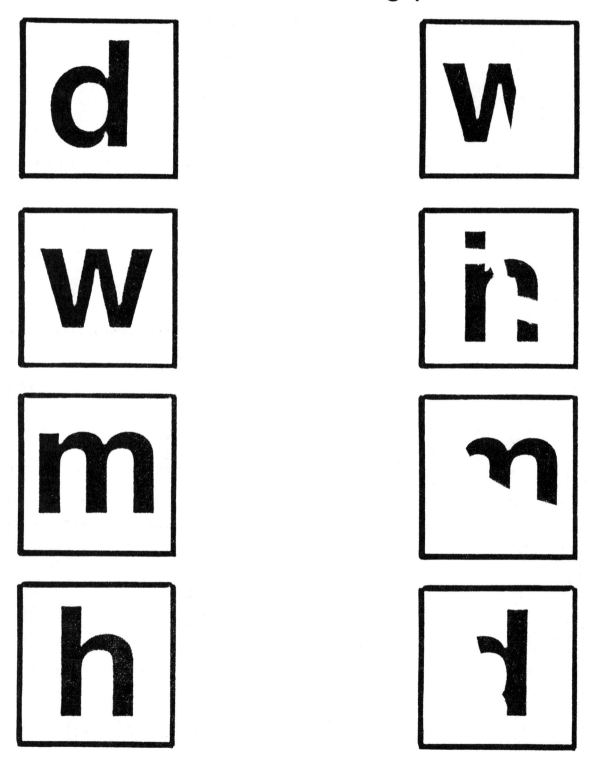

Circle the letter in each row that will look the same as the one in the box after its missing parts are filled in. One is done for you.

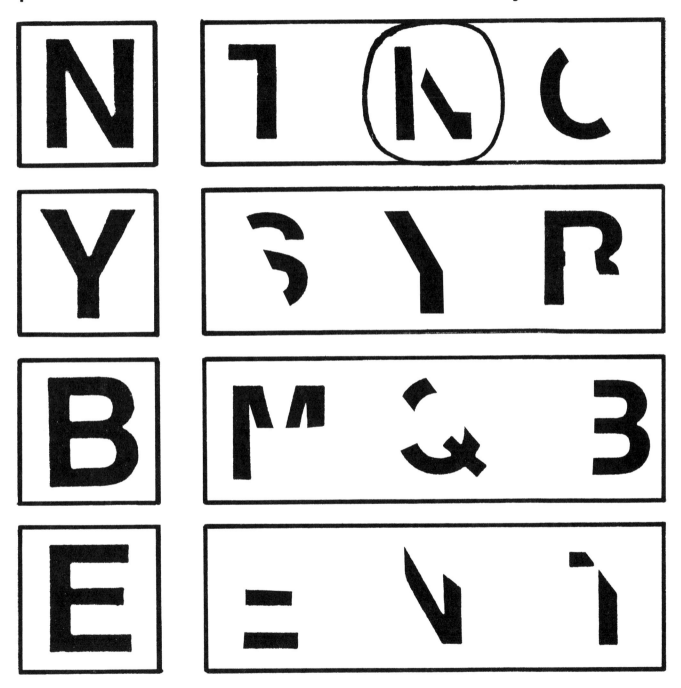

Go back and fill in the missing parts of each letter you circled.

Circle the letter in each row that will look the same as the one in the box after its missing parts are filled in.

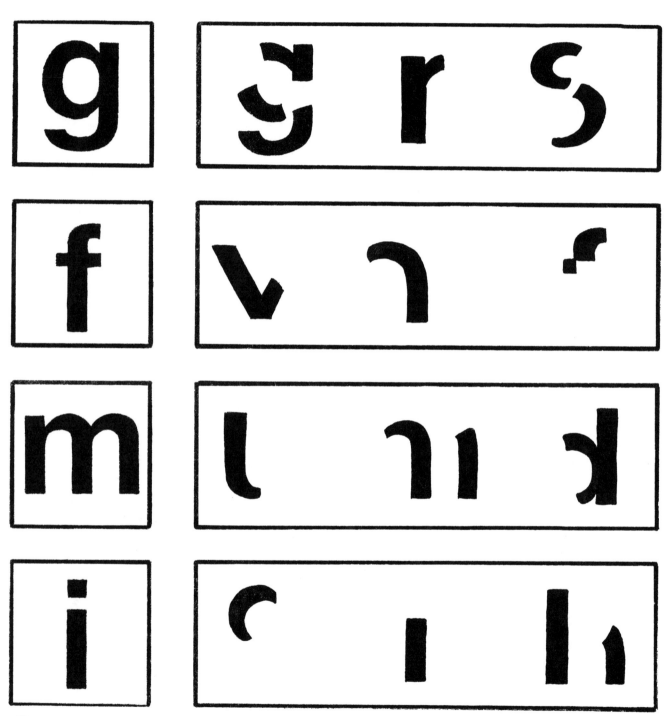

Go back and fill in the missing parts of each letter you circled.

Find all the things that **end** with the letter P.
Circle them.

Draw what each person is thinking. Then draw their faces.

Look at the blots. Draw pictures in the spaces **between** the blots. Make each picture different. One is done for you.

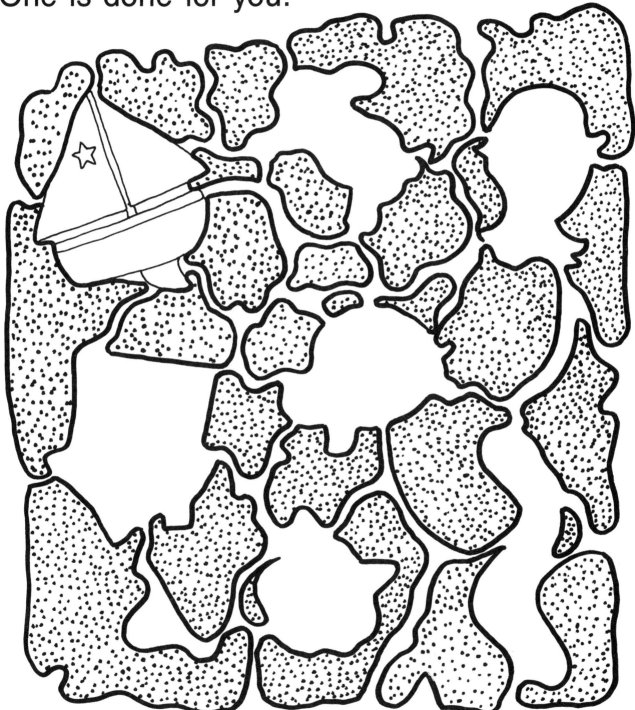

How many pictures did you draw? _____

When two things go into the Silly-Willy Machine, they come out as **one** new thing.

dog   toothbrush

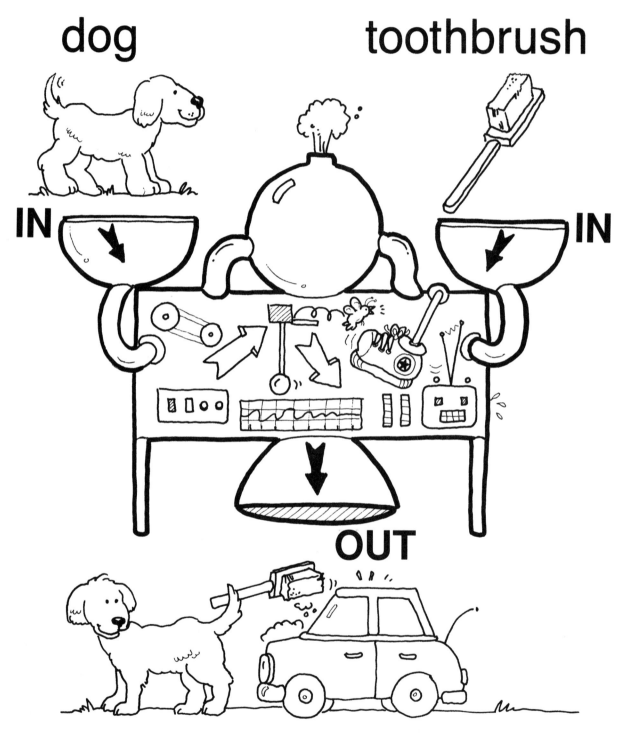

A dog and a toothbrush became a <u>car-washer</u>!

Choose two things to put into the Silly-Willy Machine. Circle them. Then draw a picture and write the name of your new invention.

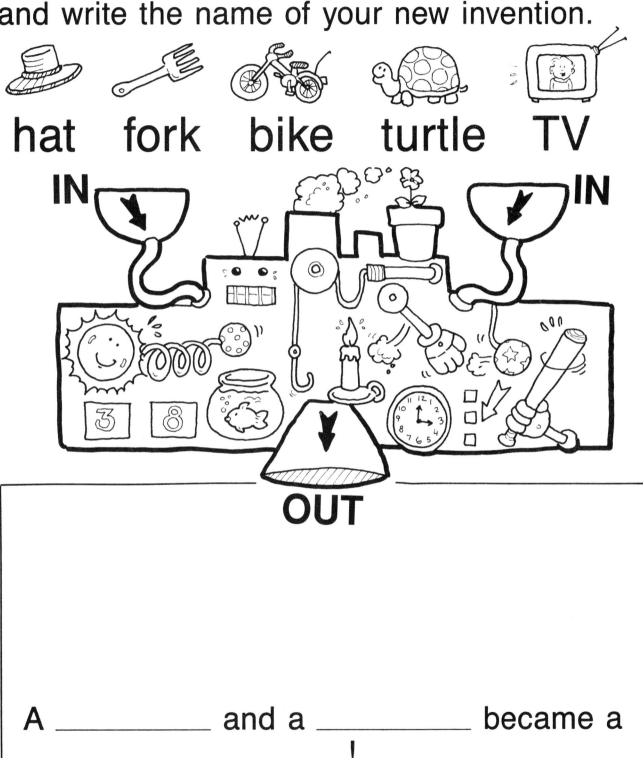

hat   fork   bike   turtle   TV

A _____ and a _____ became a
_____ _____!
_____

89

Everything is wrong in Looneyville. The Loonies like it that way! Today the mayor is mad because some things are **right**.

Find and circle the things that you think are **right** in Looneyville today!

Here are more blots! Draw pictures in between them.

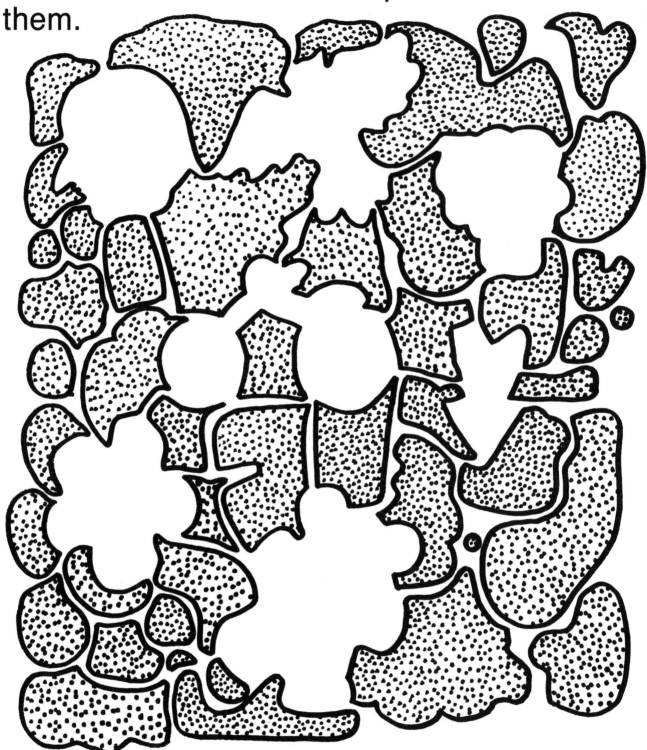

How many different pictures did you draw?

Look at all the pictures one at a time. When you think you can remember them all, turn the page.

Find the pictures you saw on the page before. Circle **only** those pictures.

Now turn back and check. Did you remember them all?

There is a frog in your pocket! How can you get it out – <u>without using your hands?</u> Draw a picture to show what you could do.